Sources
Biographies

Maureen Lewis

Published by HarperCollins*Publishers* Limited
77-85 Fulham Palace Road
Hammersmith
London
W6 8JB

www.**Collins**Education.com
Online support for schools and colleges

© HarperCollins*Publishers* Limited 2002
First published 2002

Reprinted 10 9 8 7 6 5 4 3 2 1

ISBN 0 00 713838 5

British Library Cataloguing in Publication Data
A Catalogue record for this book is available from the British Library.

Series editor: Maureen Lewis
Creative director: Louise Morely
Designer: Janet McCallum
Editor: Jo Kemp
Cover photographs: Mary Evans Picture Library T; Steve Lumb Photography L; Museum of London C; Historical Newspaper Loan Service B
Photographs: Steve Lumb Photography pp.1, 5T, 7T, 8B, 14, 29
Illustration: Clive Goodyear (Beehive Illustration) p.17C

The publishers would like to thank the following for permission to use photographs: Corbis p. 6T; Associated Press pp.6B (Ron Edmonds), 8T (Steven Senne), 13; Popperfoto pp.9T, B, 10B (Jeff Christensen/Reuters), 20T, B, 22; Hulton Archive/Deborah Feingold p.10T; TIME magazine p.11; Mary Evans Picture Library pp.15T, B, 16B, 17, 18L, R, 19TL; National Portrait Gallery p.16T; Museum of London p. 19TR, B; State Library of South Australia p.21; NASA pp. 25, 26, 27; Historical Newspaper Loan Service p.28T

Every effort has been made to trace copyright holders and to obtain their permission for the use of copyright material. The author and publishers will gladly receive any information enabling them to rectify any error or omission in subsequent editions.

Printed by Printing Express Ltd, Hong Kong

You might also like to visit
www.**fire**and**water**.co.uk
The book lover's website

Contents

Writing a biography

If you visit your local library and look in the biography section you will find many shelves filled with books written about the lives of famous, and not so famous, people.

Many readers are fascinated by the lives of other people – how they grew up and how they lived their lives. In order to write a biography an author has to undertake research into the life of the person they are going to write about.

The author will talk to the person's friends and relatives and other people who knew them. They will read any diaries and letters they can find; watch videos or television programmes about the person; visit their house and their grave; find out about their time in school and their working life; read any newspaper articles or books about them and track down any official documents like birth certificates. If the person is still alive the author will try to interview them. If the person lived in a different era or country, the author will research what it was like to live in that place at that time. A good biographer will try to find out as much as they can from as many different sources as possible. Sometimes they will even write letters to newspapers or put advertisements in magazines asking for any information.

In this book you will find some examples of the kind of materials authors might look at before they write a biography. There are also suggestions for where you can find out more about each of the featured people, if you are inspired to undertake further biographical research on them.

Biographies can be written long after someone has died or whilst they are still alive.

■ **READERS' REQUESTS**

For a biography of Varina Howell Davis (1826–1906), Mrs Jefferson Davis, who lived in London 1868-1870 and 1876–1877, would be grateful for any letters, photos or personal recollections that may be in private hands.

Joan Cash, joanc@osu.edu, Dept of History, Ohio State University, Columbus OH 43210 USA

I am writing a biography of the late anthropologist and writer, Ashley Montagu (Oxford Unitversity Press). I would appreciate contact from individuals who have correspondence or other materials that might be relevant. Susan Sperling, 1544 Lincoln Street, Berkley, CA 94703, USA. E-mail: ssperling@earthlink.net

---

You can advertise in magazines for information for your biography.

Ruby **Bridges**

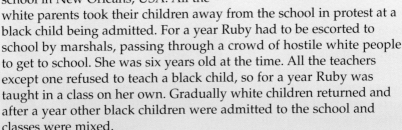

Dates: born 1954

Nationality: American

Biographical details:
In 1960 Ruby Bridges was the first black child to attend a previously "whites only" school in New Orleans, USA. All the white parents took their children away from the school in protest at a black child being admitted. For a year Ruby had to be escorted to school by marshals, passing through a crowd of hostile white people to get to school. She was six years old at the time. All the teachers except one refused to teach a black child, so for a year Ruby was taught in a class on her own. Gradually white children returned and after a year other black children were admitted to the school and classes were mixed.

Achievements:
By refusing to be intimidated, Ruby and her parents helped the Black Civil Rights Movement achieve the desegregation of schools in the southern states of America. Ruby now talks to school children and others about these events.

President Clinton presents Ruby Bridges with a Presidential Citizens' Medal during a ceremony at the White House, 8 January 2001. The award was esablished by President Nixon in 1969 to recognize exemplary service by any citizen.

INTERVIEWER: And your own family paid a price. Right?

RUBY BRIDGES HALL: Oh, definitely. My father…lost his job. He came home one night and said that his boss said he could no longer keep him there working….because there was too much pressure. Everybody knew that it was his daughter that was going to this white school, and so he had to fire him.

INTERVIEWER: Even your grandparents suffered.

RUBY BRIDGES HALL: My grandparents, who were sharecroppers in Mississippi at the time, had been living there for 25 years on this farm, and they had to leave Mississippi.

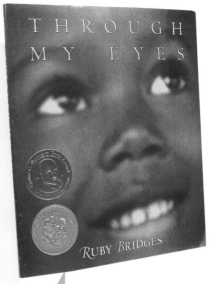

The story from Ruby's point of view

From an interview with Ruby from Online Newshour, *18 February 1997*

CHARLES BURKS, U.S. Marshal (Ret.): We expected a lot of trouble, but as it turned out, it wasn't nearly as bad as we thought, even though Miss Bridges probably thought it was. For a little girl six years old going into a strange school with four strange deputy marshals, a place she had never been before, she showed a lot of courage. She never cried. She didn't whimper. She just marched along like a little soldier. And we're all very proud of her. (applause)

From an interview from Online Newshour *with one of the marshals who took Ruby to school each day*

For a whole year I was her only teacher... The only people we saw were the federal marshals in the doorway... Ruby and I sat side by side and read together... sang together, did art together, did jumping jacks together, because it was too dangerous to go outside. The first-grade teacher who was supposed to teach her resigned rather than teach a black child, and also stripped bare the classroom... so as not to leave anything nice behind...

▼ *Barbara Henry was Ruby's teacher in 1960.*

"

Ruby's prayer

Please God, try to forgive those people
Because even if they say those bad things,
They don't know what they are doing.
So you could forgive them
Just like you did those folks a long time ago
When they said terrible things about you.

"

▼ *Six-year-old Ruby said this prayer to herself as she walked through the angry mob each day.*

Summary

This is the true story of the young child who led the cause of racial integration in Louisiana's school system. Relevant not just from the standpoint of "Black history", Ruby's strength of character in someone so young is inspiring. It's a quality family film.

USA
90 minutes
Studio/distributor:
Buena Vista

Ruby was able to attend the school because the Supreme Court had ruled that black children had the right to go to white only schools. This ruling came in 1954 but took a long time to be implemented.

This is what the court said:

> On May 17, 1954, the Supreme Court ruled in a unanimous decision that the "separate but equal" clause was unconstitutional because it violated the children's 14th amendment rights by separating them solely on the classification of the colour of their skin. Chief Justice Warren delivered the court's opinion, stating that "segregated schools are not equal and cannot be made equal, and hence they are deprived of the equal protection of the laws." This ruling in favour of integration was one of the most significant strides America has taken in favour of civil liberties.

There were equal rights demonstrations in many parts of America at the time. This one took place in New York in 1963.

Governor of Alabama George Wallace, one of the chief spokesmen for school segregation: "I draw the line in the dust and toss the gauntlet before the feet of tyranny and I say segregation now, segregation tomorrow, segregation forever." (Inaugural address, Jan. 14, 1963)

Find out more about the court case at
http://www.digisys.net/users/hootie/brown/case.htm

Bill **Gates**

Dates: born 1955

Nationality: American

Biographical details:
One of three children, Bill Gates was born in Seattle in Washington State, USA. His father is an attorney (a type of lawyer) and his mother was a teacher. He began programming computers at the age of 13.

In 1973, Gates entered Harvard University where he developed a version of the computer programming language BASIC for the first microcomputer.

Gates left Harvard to develop Microsoft, a company he had begun in 1975. He believed that computers would soon become a valuable tool in every office and in every home, so the company began developing software for personal computers.

He was married in 1994 and has two children.

Achievements:
Bill Gates has made Microsoft the biggest software company in the world.

He has written two bestselling books and has donated the proceeds of both to non-profit organizations that support the use of technology in education and skills development.

He and his wife, Melinda, have started a foundation to support projects in global health and learning.

The Private World of **BILL GATES**

A surprising visit with the man who is shaping our future

When Bill Gates was in the sixth grade*, his parents decided he needed counselling. He was at war with his mother Mary, an outgoing woman who harboured the belief that he should do what she told him. She would call him to dinner from his basement bedroom, which she had given up trying to make him clean, and he wouldn't respond.

"What are you doing?" she once demanded over the intercom.

"I'm thinking," he shouted back.

"You're thinking?"

"Yes, Mom, I'm thinking," he said fiercely. "Have you ever tried thinking?"

The psychologist they sent him to "was a really cool guy," Gates recalls. "He gave me books to read after each session, Freud stuff, and I really got into psychology theory." After a year of sessions and a battery of tests, the counsellor reached his conclusion. "You're going to lose," he told Mary. "You had better just adjust to it because there's no use trying to beat him." Mary was strong-willed and intelligent herself, her husband recalls, "but she came around to accepting that it was futile trying to compete with him."

From an article in TIME *magazine, 13 January 1997.*

* Children in the sixth grade are 11–12 years old.

The first Microsoft advertisement, 1976

A Microsoft advertisement from 2001

Pie in the face

BILL GATES received a pie in the face as he entered a meeting hosted by Flemish Minister and President Van den Brande. Gates responded mildly, saying the pie "just wasn't that good." Says Noel Godin, "This man told us he really loved Gates in the past, saying that he was very cool and passionate. But little by little he considered that his power had tainted him, and that he was becoming more and more haughty with his own collaborators. So the man who gave us the information considered, and he's not alone, that it wouldn't be bad to teach Bill a lesson, to bring him back to reality. That's how he explained to us why he was doing it. He's far from being a member of our band, he's not an anarchist and he likes his work with Microsoft, but he thought it had to happen."

Bill Gates Personal Wealth Clock

just a small portion of <u>Why Bill Gates is Richer than You</u> by <u>Philip Greenspun</u>

Wed Nov 7 03:27:13 EST 2001

Microsoft Stock Price:	$64.78
Bill Gates's Wealth:	$73.154800 billion
U.S. Population:	285,501,502
Your Personal Contribution:	**$256.233**

There is a site on the Internet that updates this "clock" every day so you can check how rich he is. Visit it at www.webho.com/WealthClock

Bill Gates's personal vision of the future

Emmeline **Pankhurst**

Dates: 1858–1928

Nationality: British

Biographical details:
Emmeline Pankhurst is famous for her efforts trying to get the government to allow women in Britain to vote. She was born in England at a time when women had few rights. Married women were not even allowed to have property of their own – everything they had was owned by their husbands.

Emmeline founded the Woman's Social and Political Union (WSPU) in 1903. Other women soon joined her cause. The group did everything they could to make life difficult for the politicians of the day. Members were frequently sent to prison because of their actions. In the year 1908–09 Pankhurst was sent to prison three times. She was sent to prison 12 more times in the year 1912–13 and served a total of about 30 days.

During World War I Emmeline visited the USA, Canada and Russia to encourage women to take work in the factories.

Achievements:
Emmeline Pankhurst's 40 years of fighting were finally successful in the year she died. The Representation of the People Act was passed in 1928. This gave the vote equally to men and women in Britain.

Emmeline Pankhurst being arrested

15

Emmeline
Pankhurst by
Georgina
Brackenbury

The women who were
campaigning for equal rights with
men had their own newspaper
which they sold on the streets.

Emmeline and Christabel
Pankhurst, and another
suffragette, Flora Drummond,
at Bow Street Magistrate's
Court.

Extracts from Emmeline
Pankhurst's autobiograohy My
Own Story. The Museum of
London holds a copy of the book.

[1st extract]

It was a custom of my father and mother to make the round of our bedrooms every night before going themselves to bed. When they entered my room that night I was still awake, but for some reason I chose to pretend I was asleep. My father bent over me, shielding the candle flame with his big hand. I cannot know exactly what I thought was in his mind as he gazed down at me, but I heard him say, somewhat sadly, "What a pity she wasn't born a lad."

My first hot impulse was to sit up in bed and protest that I didn't want to be a boy, but I lay still and heard my parents' footsteps pass on toward the next child's bed. I thought about my father's remark for many days afterward…It was made quite clear that men considered themselves superior to women, and that women accepted this situation. I found this view of things difficult to reconcile with the fact that both my father and my mother were advocates of women having the vote.

[2nd extract]

The education of boys was considered a much more serious matter than the education of girls. My parents…discussed the question of my brothers' education as a matter of real importance. My education and that of my sister were scarcely discussed at all. Of course we went to a carefully selected girls' school, but beyond the facts that the headmistress was a good woman and that all the pupils were girls of my own class, nobody seemed concerned. A girl's education at that time seemed to have for its prime object the art of "making a home attractive".

THE GOVERNMENT'S METHODS OF BARBARISM.

FORCIBLE FEEDING IN PRISON.

In some cases, instead of nasal feeding as in the picture, the still more dangerous practice of feeding through the mouth, by a tube, down the throat, is adopted. This was done in the case of Jane Warton.

(This Cartoon is being made into a Poster, which can be obtained separately. Particulars will be found on page 274.)

Emmeline Pankhurst was sent to prison many times for campaigning for women's rights. While in prison many of the suffragettes went on hunger strike. Emily went on hunger strike ten times but was never force fed as some women were. Sometimes she was so weak from hunger striking that when she was released from prison she had to be carried to meetings on a stretcher.

An account, by Constance Lytton, of being force fed in prison

Two of the wardresses took hold of my arms, one held my head and one my feet. The doctor leant on my knees as he stooped over my chest to get at my mouth. I shut my mouth and clenched my teeth… The doctor seemed annoyed at my resistance and he broke into a temper as he pried my teeth with the steel implement. The pain was intense and at last I must have given way, for he got the gap between my teeth, when he proceeded to turn it until my jaws were fastened wide apart. Then he put down my throat a tube, which seemed to me much too wide and something like four feet in length. I choked the moment it touched my throat. Then the food was poured in quickly; it made me sick a few seconds after it was down. I was sick all over the doctor and wardresses. As the doctor left he gave me a slap on the cheek. Presently the wardresses left me. Before long I heard the sounds of the forced feeding in the next cell to mine. It was almost more than I could bear, it was Elsie Howley. When the ghastly process was over and all quiet, I tapped on the wall and called out at the top of my voice, "No Surrender", and then came the answer in Elsie's voice, "No Surrender".

Suffragette badges

A suffragette poster of the time

Two of Emmeline's daughters were active campaigners with their mother. Both finally left Britain but continued to work for women's rights. Sylvia emigrated to Australia and Christabel to California, USA.

Donald **Bradman**

Dates: 1908–2001

Nationality: Australian

Biographical details:
Donald Bradman was born in Cootamundra, New South Wales, Australia, and was the youngest of five children. He came from a keen cricketing family and played from a very young age. He claimed to have trained his eye by hitting a golf ball against a steel water tank

He played in his first match at the age of 11, scoring his first century (100 runs) when he was 12.

Bradman toured England for the first time in 1930. He scored 334 in one innings, which was a record for test (internatonal) cricket.

In 1948 Bradman was captain of the Australian team that beat England by four matches to nil. He retired from first-class cricket in 1949 and was knighted in the same year, becoming Sir Donald Bradman.

Achievements:
Bradman played 80 test series for Australia, many of them as Captain. His career total was 211 centuries and he scored 6996 runs in Test cricket. His test average is 99.94 runs, by far the highest ever.

Bat used by Bradman in Australia v. England Test, Leeds 1930

ADELAIDE, 26 February 2001

SIR DONALD BRADMAN DEAD

AUSTRALIA WAS IN mourning today following the death of Sir Donald Bradman, regarded by many as the world's greatest cricketer.

Sir Donald died peacefully in his sleep at his Adelaide home yesterday, aged 92, said Richard Mulvaney of the Bradman Museum. He had been in poor health and was trying to recover from a bout of pneumonia. "I believe he died peacefully in his sleep and his family were there not long after," Mr Mulvaney said. "He was suffering from pneumonia before Christmas and was hospitalised for a short period, went home before Christmas and was really trying to recover."

Tributes immediately began pouring in for Australia's finest batsman. A visibly saddened Prime Minister John Howard expressed sympathy to his family on behalf of all Australia. Mr Howard said he had visited Sir Donald a little over a week ago in Adelaide and said he had been "very ill".

"It was always going to be a shock when Don Bradman died because he has really been the most dominant figure in Australian life now for decades," he told ABC radio. Mr Howard said he had spoken to Sir Donald's son John this morning to express sympathy on behalf of all of Australia, send our love to the Bradman family and record the appreciation of the Australian people for a wonderful life. It had not only given this country and the world the greatest cricketer but, according to many people who compare these things, perhaps the greatest sportsman in 100 years.

Mr Mulvaney said there was no question Sir Donald was the greatest batsman who ever lived. In 52 Test matches from 1928 to 1948, he scored 6996 runs at an average of 99.94. His average is expected never to be bettered. "Any cricket lover or, in fact, any Australian and in fact many people around the world will certainly mourn Sir Donald's passing," Mr Mulvaney said.

Sir Donald was born at Cootamundra in southern New South Wales on August 27 1908, but grew up in the southern highlands town of Bowral, about 100 km south-west of Sydney. He married his wife Jessie Menzies in 1932 and the couple lived together for 65 years in the same home in Adelaide. However, Sir Donald felt increasingly lonely after her death from cancer in 1997. Sir Donald is survived by the couple's two children, John and Shirley.

Following his retirement from first-class cricket in 1949, Sir Donald became an Australian selector and served two three-year terms as chairman of the Australian Cricket Board.

Former test skipper Mark Taylor said Sir Donald was the greatest Australian he had ever met. "Fifty-three years after playing his final Test match, he was still revered around the world, held in incredible esteem. As a cricketer, the world has known no equal. He was the true symbol of fine sportsmanship, the benchmark that all young cricketers aspired to. His innings may have closed but his legacy will forever live on in the hearts of millions of Australians." South Australian Premier John Olsen said Sir Donald would be given a state funeral in Adelaide if his family agreed.

SIR DONALD BRADMAN

Career Statistics

Career Record

	Innings	Not Out Score	Highest	Runs	Average
All Matches	669	107	452	50 731	90.27
All First Class	338	43	452	28 067	95.1
Second Class	331	64	320	22 664	84.8
All Test Matches	80	10	334	6 996	99.94
Sheffield Shield	96	15	452	8 926	110.19
Grade Matches	93	17	303	6 598	86.8
Test vs England	63	7	334	5 028	89.78

HIGHEST AVERAGE OF
ANY BATSMAN – MORE
THAN 50% BETTER

Methods of Dismissal

Number of innings	669
Caught	340
Bowled	148
Not Out	107
L.B.W.	37
Stumped	14
Hit Wicket	1

Number of Centuries

All Matches	211
All First Class	117
All Second Class	29
Test vs England	19
Sheffield Shield	36
Grade	28

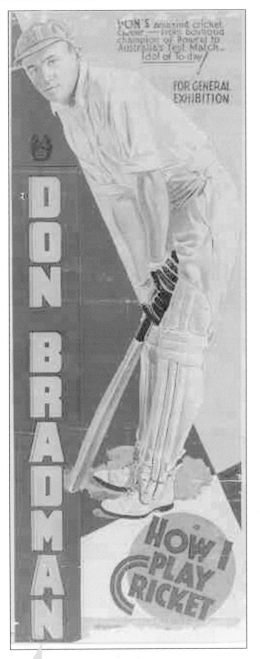

A poster for the 1930s film Donald Bradman – How I Play Cricket

Shown on Australian free-to-air TV on Wednesday 29 May, 1996 in conjunction with a fund-raising telethon in aid of the Bradman Trust for the development of cricket in Australia.

Interview conducted by Ray Martin. Transcribed by Steve Thompson.

RM: Sir Donald, thanks for your time… thanks for talking to me.

DB: Pleasure.

RM: In 30 years I've interviewed princes and presidents, prime ministers… why am I nervous?

DB: I don't think you are. I'm the one that's nervous, not you.

RM: But when I told people I'd be talking to you, they said almost to a man and a woman, that's fantastic, half your luck. Do you realize that you're not just respected, but deeply loved here in Australia?

DB: No, no, I don't look at it that way at all. I'm just an ordinary human being.

RM: Is that why you haven't spoken to anyone for so long?

DB: Ooh, I've spoken to a lot of people, but not publicly. I don't like publicity of any kind, never have done. And I like it less as I get older.

Neil **Armstrong**

Dates: born 1930

Nationality: American

Biographical details:
Neil Armstrong joined the US Navy and was a naval aviator from 1949 to 1952. He went on to join NASA as a civilian test pilot. He has a BSc degree and an MSc degree.

Armstrong was selected as an astronaut in 1962 and made his first space flight in 1966. On 16 July 1969 the Apollo 11 spacecraft left Earth for the Moon. On board were Neil Armstrong, Buzz Aldrin and Mike Collins. Four days later Neil and Buzz landed on the Moon's surface while Collins circled the Moon in the command module. When Neil stepped out of the landing craft he said, "One small step for man, one giant leap for mankind." He left NASA in 1971 and became a businessman.

Achievements:
Neil Armstrong was the first man to step onto the moon.

KSC Home Page   Site Search   FAQ   Site Survey   Customer Forum   NASA Centers   Privacy Statement

Apollo Information

Home

Goals

Spacecraft

Flight Summary

Unmanned Saturn Missions

Unmanned Apollo-Saturn Missions

Manned Missions

Apollo 11 *(Columbia and Eagle)*
Saturn V
July 16-24, 1969
Neil A. Armstrong, Michael Collins, Edwin E. Aldrin, Jr.

08 days, 03 hours, 18 minutes
First manned lunar landing mission and lunar surface EVA.
"Houston, Tranquility base here. The eagle has landed."
– July 20th, 1969
Landing site: Sea of Tranquility.
Landing Coordinates: 0.71 degrees North, 23.63 degrees East

1 EVA of 02 hours, 31 minutes. Flag and instruments deployed; unveiled plaque on the LM descent stage with inscription: "Here Men From Planet Earth First Set Foot Upon the Moon. July 1969 A.D. We Came In Peace For All Mankind." Lunar surface stay time 21.6 hours; 59.5 hours in lunar orbit, with 30 orbits. LM ascent stage left in lunar orbit. 20 kg (44 lbs) of material gathered.

Section from NASA webpages:
Flight summary

Apollo 11 badge ◄

ARMSTRONG: In the final phases of the descent after a number of program alarms, we looked at the landing area and found a very large crater. This is the area we decided we would not go into; we extended the range downrange. The exhaust dust was kicked up by the engine and this caused some concern in that it degraded our ability to determine not only our altitude in the final phases but also our translational velocities over the ground. It's quite important not to stub your toe during the final phases of touchdown.

From the space-to-ground tapes:

EAGLE: 540 feet, down at 30 [feet per second] . . . down at 15 . . . 400 feet down at 9 . . . forward . . . 350 feet, down at 4 . . . 300 feet, down 3 1/2 . . . 47 forward . . . 1 1/2 down . . . 13 forward . . . 11 forward? coming down nicely . . . 200 feet, 4 1/2 down . . . 5 1/2 down . . . 5 percent . . . 75 feet . . . 6 forward . . . lights on . . . down 2 1/2 . . . 40 feet? down 2 1/2, kicking up some dust . . . 30 feet, 2 1/2 down . . . faint shadow . . . 4 forward . . . 4 forward . . . drifting to right a little . . . O.K. . . .

HOUSTON: 30 seconds [fuel remaining].

EAGLE: Contact light! O.K., engine stop . . . descent engine command override off . . .

HOUSTON: We copy you down, Eagle.

EAGLE: Houston, Tranquility Base here. The Eagle has landed!

HOUSTON: Roger, Tranquility. We copy you on the ground. You've got a bunch of guys about to turn blue. We're breathing again. Thanks a lot.

Recollections and transcript from NASA official archive

Commemorative plaque fixed to the leg of the luna landing vehicle

The Moon walk made headlines all over the world.

ASTRONAUT HALL OF FAME

Hall of Fame Info
Space Camp Info
Field Trip Info
The Astronauts
Shop Our Store
The Launch Pad
Calendar
The Newsroom
Make Contact
Links
Home

NeilArmstrong

Neil A. Armstrong commanded the Gemini 8 mission and became the first human to walk on the moon as commander of Apollo 11.

He was born in Wapakoneta, Ohio, on August 5, 1930. He received a Bachelor of Science degree in aeronautical engineering from Purdue University and a Master of Science degree from the University of Southern California.

Armstrong joined the Navy and flew as a naval aviator from 1949 to 1952. In 1955 he joined the National Advisory Committee for Aeronautics' Lewis Flight Propulsion Laboratory and later transferred to the High Speed Flight Station at Edwards Air Force Base, California, as a civilian aeronautical test research pilot for NACA and NASA. Among the aircraft he tested was the X-15 rocket plane…

Armstrong left NASA in 1971 and became a professor of aeronautical engineering at the University of Cincinnati, where he taught until 1981. He has since been in the business world and he currently is chairman of CTA, Inc.

Neil Armstrong was inducted into the Astronaut Hall of Fame on March 19, 1993.

The start and the finish of the biography of Neil Armstrong to be found in the Astronaunt Hall of Fame website

Many authors have written biographies of Armstrong.

For all mankind: A Unique Space adventure

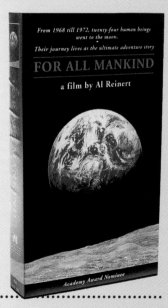

Edition Details:
- PAL format
- Surround Sound, Colour, PAL
- ASIN: B00004CM85
- Catalogue Number: IWCV1006

★★★★★ **The Best Archival Footage**,
15 December, 2000
Reviewer: **A viewer** from Hampshire,
England
Using original (and often previously unseen)
NASA archival footage, we hear what it was
like to "be there" from the astronauts
themselves, with no intrusive and
unnecessary voiceovers. The evocative and
haunting music is by Brian Eno. This is the
closest you will get to feeling what it was
actually like. A wonderful film in the fullest
sense of the word.

Sources and further research suggestions

Ruby Bridges

Sources of the items on pages 6–9
Through my Eyes by Ruby Bridges, Scholastic, Inc; ISBN: 0590189239
Transcript of the interview with the marshal and with Ruby herself from Online Newshour, 18 February 1997
www.pbs.org/newshour/bb/race_relations/jan-june97/bridges_2-18.html
Account from Ruby's teacher on the townonline website
www.townonline.com/metro/wellesley/03570470.htm
Video not currently available in the UK
Details of the court case from
www.digisys.net/users/hootie/brown/case.htm
Further sources
What a Hero! by David Orme and Helen Bird, 2002 in this series
The Story of Ruby Bridges by Robert Coles, New York: Scholastic 1995
Driftwood Newscope, "Still I Rise: Ruby Bridges' Fate"
www.uno.edu/~drif/1997/feb6/ruby.htm
The Marshals' Moniter, "Ruby Bridges becomes an honourable deputy"
www.usdoj.gov/marshals/monitor/sep-2000/ruby.html
The official Ruby Bridges website www.rubybridges.net

Bill Gates

Sources of the items on pages 10–14
Biographical Dictionary of Recent Times by David Orme and Helen Bird, 2002 in this series
TIME magazine article 13 January 1997. Available on
www.time.com/time/gates/gates2.html
"Pie in the face" text from www.zpub.com/un/bill/
Bill Gates Personal Wealth from www.webho.com/WealthClock
The Road Ahead by Bill Gates, Penguin Books; ISBN: 0140243518
Further sources
Information about Microsoft on the official website www.microsoft.com
The life of Bill Gates is on the site at www.microsoft.com/billgates/bio.asp
Bill Gates by Sean Connolly, Heinemann Profiles 1998
Bill Gates by Richard Wood, Hodder Wayland 2001

Emmeline Pankhurst

Sources of the items on pages 15–19
Biographical Dictionary of Recent Times by David Orme and Helen Bird, 2002 in this series
The National Portrait Gallery's three pictures of Emmeline Pankhurst can be viewed on www.npg.org.uk
Constantce Lytton's account of force feeding is taken from her book *Prison and Prisoners*
The cartoon of force feeding and the poster of John Bull's umbrella are all to be found on www.spartacus.schoolnet.co.uk/Whunger
My Own Story by Emmeline Pankhurst, Greenwood Press, London; ISBN: 0313249261

Further sources
Pictures of the suffragette movement www.flyinglemon.com/breadandroses/index
Biographies of the Pankhurst family www.xrefer.com/entry/360467
For a timeline showing when women got the vote in countries around the world
visit www.womenshistory.about.com/library/weekly/aa091600a.htm It runs from
1881 (when Scottish women got the vote) to1994 (when black women in South
Africa got the vote)
Livewire Real Lives: *Emmeline Pankhurst* by Sandra Woodcock, Hodder and
Stoughton 1998
Emmeline Pankhurst by Margaret Hudson, Heinemann Library 1998

Donald **Bradman**

Sources of the items on pages 21–24
Biographical Dictionary of Recent Times by David Orme and Helen Bird, 2002 in this
series
Obituary from www.the pavilion.com.au/international/200102
Career statistics www.pnc.com.au/~scurry/stats.htm
Film poster *Donald Bradman – How I Play Cricket* can be seen on
www.slsa.sa.gov.au/library/collres/bradman/images/poster.jpg
Interview from
www.cricket.org/link_to_database/PLAYERS/A…/BRADMAN_INTERVIEW

Further sources
The State Library of South Australia has the Bradman Digital Library. You can visit
it on www.bradman.sa.com.au/
The Bradman Museum is at www.bradman.org.au/

Neil **Armstrong**

Sources of the items on pages 25–29
Biographical Dictionary of Recent Times by David Orme and Helen Bird, 2002 in this
series
Transcript from space to ground tapes, interviews with the astronauts and
photographs can be found on the NASA website at
www.ksc.nasa.gov/history/apollo/apollo-11/apollo-11.html
A biography of Neil Armstrong is to be found in the Astronaunt Hall of Fame
www.astronauts.org/austronauts/armstrong.htm
Neil Armstrong by Mike Goldsmith, Hodder Wayland 2001; ISBN: 0750233575
One Giant Leap: The Story of Neil Armstrong by Don Brown, Houghton Mifflin
Company 2001; ISBN: 0618152393
Video *For All Mankind: A Unique Space Adventure* available in the UK, ASIN:
B00004CM85, Catalogue Number: IWCV1006

Further sources
Neil Armstrong: The First Man on The Moon by Barbara Kramer Enslow Publishers
1997; ISBN: 0894908286
Neil Armstrong: A Space Biography by Carmen Bresdeson, Enslow Publishers 1998;
ISBN: 0894909738
Neil Armstrong by Sean Connolly, Heinemann Profiles 1999
Video *Apollo – One Giant Leap For Mankind*. Available in UK.ASIN: B00004CYG1,
Catalogue Number: DD2903
Details of space equipment can be found on www.astronauts.org/spaceshop

Index